THE RACE TO THE SOUTH POLE

BY LINDA YOSHIZAWA

MODERN CURRICULUM PRESS

Pearson Learning Group

In 1909, the world learned exciting news. Robert Peary and Matthew Henson became the first people to reach the North Pole. Most people were thrilled by the news. One person was not.

Roald Amundsen

That person was a Norwegian explorer named Roald Amundsen. He too had been preparing an expedition to the North Pole. He had planned to earn his place in history by conquering the pole. He had planned to use the fame he would earn to get out of debt. Peary and Henson's success had dashed Amundsen's hopes.

Amundsen quickly came up with a new plan. He would be first to reach the South Pole instead. However, he was afraid that his supporters would withdraw their money when they learned he had changed his plan. So Amundsen kept his idea a secret from everyone but his brother and the ship's captain. Of course, keeping the secret from his backers also meant keeping it from the rest of the world.

Keeping the plan secret was an odd choice. It was interesting because at that time explorers from several countries were announcing plans to join the race to the South Pole. Explorers from the United States, Germany, and Great Britain had already made such announcements.

On August 9, 1910, Amundsen's ship, the *Fram*, left Christiana, Norway, which is now Oslo. Amundsen's original plans called for him to cut across the Atlantic at Spain, and then head north toward the Arctic. But on September 6, just three hours before the *Fram* was set to depart, Amundsen met with his crew. Pointing to a map of Antarctica, he explained his plan to head south instead of north. The crew members were stunned. But they agreed to the change.

The crew probably went along with Amundsen because they knew he was so experienced in polar travel. And he had prepared so well for a strenuous cold-weather adventure.

Amundsen had been to Antarctica before. In 1895, he had been on the first ship ever to land on the continent. He and his crew were excellent skiers. He took three or four back-ups for every important piece of equipment. And he chose approximately one hundred Arctic dogs to pull the heavy sleds that would carry all of his supplies. The dogs even responded to Amundsen's whistled commands. Amundsen knew that the success of his trip rested largely on having strong, healthy, and well-trained dogs.

Amundsen arrived at the Ross Ice Shelf at Antarctica on January 14, 1911. The crew immediately began to build a camp on the Bay of Whales. They set up living structures and carried in supplies. Amundsen had chosen the site carefully. It was easy to reach and was filled with animals that the crew could hunt for food.

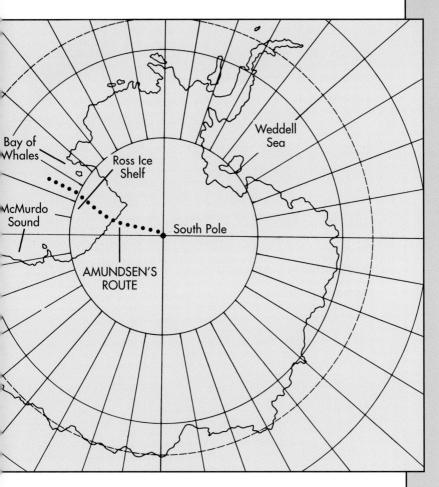

Antarctica

Amundsen and his crew put the sled dogs to work right away. In three weeks, the men and dogs had completed the strenuous job of moving ten tons of supplies to the camp.

Amundsen made clever rules to help his crew survive a cold winter in a small camp during the sunless days and nights. He gave each man a special job. Then he set up a schedule. Every day the crew would get up at 7:30 and eat breakfast together. The men would work from 9:00 to 5:15, with a lunch break from 12:00 to 2:00.

Their jobs allowed the men to get away from each other and work in different parts of the camp. In the evenings, they were glad to get together again for dinner and entertainment. For fun, the crew read or played darts.

When spring and longer days of sunlight came to the southern hemisphere at the end of August, Amundsen's crew was ready to head for the pole.

But the weather was not ready for them. Strong blizzards were raging. In fact, most of the blizzards in Antarctica are not caused by falling snow. Rather, the wind is so strong at the bottom of the Earth, that it whips up snow already on the ground. Temperatures can reach as low as one hundred degrees below zero. The weather made life miserable for Amundsen and his men. Freezing wind and snow whipped around them. They had to turn back on several expeditions south. Tension begin to build as the crew waited for clear weather. But finally, on October 11, 1911, Amundsen and four of his men began the final part of the trip to the South Pole.

The weather was not terrible at first. They could sometimes travel as far as twenty miles a day. Then, just after climbing a huge glacier, they ran into a raging blizzard. To keep to their schedule and avoid using up their supplies, they kept going. For ten days they continued their strenuous journey through high winds and pounding snow.

Finally on the last dangerous part of their trek, they reached a glacier. The glacier's snow hid deep holes. But the team kept going. And finally they crossed the glacier successfully. On December 8, they moved into territory that no one else had ever explored. That was a triumph, but they still wondered if they would be the first explorers to reach the pole.

On the afternoon of December 14, 1911, they got their answer. Instruments showed that they had reached the South Pole. A thrilled Amundsen set up a tent and raised the Norwegian flag.

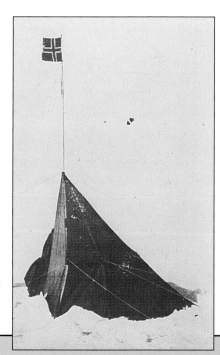

**Amundsen's Camp
at the South Pole**

Robert Falcon Scott

But Amundsen was not the only explorer on the continent at the time. In September, 1909, a British Navy captain named Robert Falcon Scott, had announced to the whole world that he would try to reach the pole. He said that the main object of the expedition would be to reach the South Pole for the honor of Great Britain. He also planned to study the animals and rocks of Antarctica.

Like Amundsen, Scott had already been to Antarctica before. On this first expedition, Scott and his crew did scientific studies and crossed into unexplored territory. He had even viewed the terrain from above—in a balloon! This group had not tried to reach the South Pole itself. But they had faced many hardships and learned ways to cope with Antarctica's miserable cold and wind.

One of the miseries Scott and his crew had faced on the first trip concerned sled dogs. Toward the end of the expedition, the dogs had died, and the men had started pulling the sleds themselves. Scott remembered having seen the dogs suffer and the agony of pulling the sleds. This experience influenced how he organized his next trip to Antarctica.

Scott gathered his ship, his crew, and his supplies. Remembering his past experience with dogs, he made different plans for this trip. He bought three motorized sleds—a new and untried invention—and nineteen white ponies. Ponies had been used successfully on another British trip to Antarctica. And Scott did not believe that dogs could be trained well enough to pull the sleds. So he took along only thirty-three dogs. This decision was disastrous. Ponies do not have enough fur to keep warm in Antarctica. And they cannot pull sleds over the rough terrain as well as dogs can.

On June 1, 1910, Scott's ship, the *Terra Nova*, left England. Like Amundsen's ship, it would make several stops before heading across the ocean to Antarctica. When the ship docked in Australia, Scott received a telegram from Amundsen. It was short and to the point. It said only "Am going south, Amundsen."

Scott was stunned. Like the rest of the world, he'd believed Amundsen's expedition was headed north to the Arctic. Now the trip to the pole was a true race, and Scott wondered how it would end.

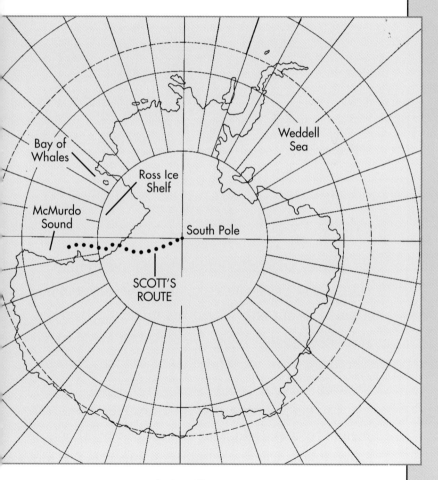

Antarctica

The *Terra Nova*

Scott's voyage had problems almost from the start. A few days out to sea, the *Terra Nova* ran into a storm. As the ship tossed and rolled, the men and animals were miserable. Water rushed into the ship. The *Terra Nova* was in danger of sinking. Though the crew saved the ship, some of the animals died.

Then, a few days after the storm, the *Terra Nova* met its first ice field. The ship sailed very slowly, as Scott did not want to collide with an iceberg. It took the ship three weeks to sail through the ice field.

Finally, on January 4, 1911, the ship reached McMurdo Sound. This was sixty miles farther from the pole than where Amundsen had landed. And a mile and a half of ice kept the ship from reaching the shore. The ship anchored. The crew began unloading supplies and carrying them across the ice. Two of the motorized sleds made it safely to shore. But the heaviest one broke through the ice and sank.

The crew was able to use the other two motorized sleds to unload the ship and set up camp. Then the men set out to leave supplies along the way in places called *depots*. One of the depots was a small cabin at Hut Point. Scott had used the hut on his earlier expedition.

This depot was close to the pole, and Scott had counted on using it. But when he arrived at the hut, he found that a simple mistake had ruined his plans. A window had been left open three years before by another expedition. Over the years, snow had drifted through the window. The hut was now filled with ice. Now the hut would be useless to Scott's party.

The crew also began to doubt that the ponies would make it through the snow. Snowshoes had been made for the ponies. However, they had lost all but one pair.

On November 1, Scott finally set out with the motorized sleds, ponies, and dogs. The group traveled at night because the ponies didn't sink as much in freezing snow. In the bitter cold, icicles often hung from the men's mustaches. The white of the sky blended with the white of the snow. This confused their senses of balance and direction. Then on December 5, the team was caught in a blizzard. For four days the men stayed inside their tents. The four-day delay meant that the men would collide with another blizzard later in the trip.

Scott and His Men at the South Pole

Almost as soon as the team started out again, another disaster occurred. The strenuous work in the ice and snow was too much for the ponies. The men ended up pulling the sleds themselves. It was slow going. On December 13, the party was able to travel only four miles.

They traveled on, with each explorer pulling 190 pounds of supplies. Still the men did not stop. But they did not know that Amundsen had already reached the pole.

For the final leg of the journey, Scott took along four men. As the party pushed ahead, they watched for signs of Amundsen. They found none, and by January 13, the men were tired but cheerful. They knew they were about to reach the pole.

As they approached the pole they suddenly spotted the signs they'd hoped not to see—a flag and a camp. Then Scott knew Amundsen had beaten him. Scott and his party reached the pole on January 17, 1912, only five weeks after Amundsen.

Disappointed, Scott and his men began the eight-hundred-mile journey back to their camp. But the hardest part of the journey was yet to come. The men were weak, sick, and suffering from frostbite. They lost their way and were unable to find where they had stored food for the return trip. Because their journey took longer than expected, the men did not have enough to eat.

Then on March 20, another blizzard hit. Trapped, sick, and with very little food, the men knew they were doomed. Despite this, Scott continued to write his thoughts in his diary and in letters until the end.

Roald Amundsen was horribly upset by the news that Scott had died. He felt that Scott's disaster would always be linked with his own achievement. History has proven him right.

It is through the writings of both Amundsen and Scott that we know so much about what happened. Their records, so clear and full of details, told the whole world the amazing story of the race to the South Pole.